The Real History of

International Women's Day

and

March 8

The Real History of International Women's Day and March 8

R. Jawahar

THE REAL HISTORY OF
INTERNATIONAL WOMEN'S DAY AND MARCH 8
R. Jawahar

First Published 2017

ISBN 978-93-5002-471-3

Published by
AAKAR BOOKS
28 E Pocket IV, Mayur Vihar Phase I, Delhi 110 091
Phones : 011 2279 5505, 2279 5641
aakarbooks@gmail.com; www.aakarbooks.com

Cover design: P. Vedarajan

Cover drawing courtesy: IWD Organising Committee, 2010, Canada

Designed by
Limited Colors, Delhi 110 092

Printed at
Sapra Brothers, Delhi 110 092

Contents

Dedicated to

Comrade **Mythily Sivaraman** (born in 1939): She was a leader of the Communist Party of India (Marxist) and Working President of the All India Democratic Women's Association. Mythily was a militant leader who worked full-time for the rights of women, workers, agricultural labourers, middle class people and the so-called untouchables. As a fine intellectual she has written extensively on various subjects. And it was she from whom I heard the word 'feminism' for the first time in the early 1970s.

Comrade **Leelavathi** (1957–1997): She was a militant working class cadre of the Communist Party of India (Marxist) and the All India Democratic Women's Association in Madurai. Leelavathi was murdered in 1997 at the age of 40 by the then state ruling party men, when she successfully fought against the water tank mafia and ensured free supply of drinking water to the people in her area.

Comrade **Renée Côté** (born in 1937): She involved herself with the American feminist movement as a "leftist feminist" (end of the 1960s, 70s and beginning of the 80s). She is the author of *La Journée internationale* des *femmes ou les vraies dates des mystérieuses origines du 8 mars jusqu'ici embrouillées, truquées, oubliées: la clef* des *énigmes. La vérité historique.* (*International Women's Day or the real dates of the mysterious origins of March 8 until now confused, fabricated, forgotten: the key to the enigmas. The historical truth*), published in 1984 (les éditions du remue-ménage,

Québec). This has been the only book on the origins of IWD and of the date March 8, as far as I have known during my research. She was a TV researcher during the 1960s in Québec and worked as a psychotherapist during the 90s in the US. She has also written the book *Was My Mother Schizophrenic?* in 2008.

Foreword

Through the pages of this significant publication, the author, comrade R. Jawahar introduces us to the real story behind arguably the most widely observed day by women across the world, International Women's Day.

Through painstaking and detailed research the author reveals the socialist origins of the observance tracing its roots to the historic days at the turn of the 20th century when the battle against capitalism was joined by militant communist women, who were fighting to ensure a more holistic and comprehensive understanding of the "woman question" in society at large and also within the communist-led movements to which they belonged.

The author correctly traces the separate circumstances of the call for the observance for an international day with the actual date of March 8 which is now recognised as the international day.

Today countries across the world observe March 8. While this is welcome, it also provides the ground for a dilution of the socialist origins of March 8, of its history as the symbol of struggles of women particularly working women in challenging exploitative capitalist structures. In India, women's struggles for justice in addition to the fight against capitalist exploitation are very closely intertwined with the struggle against casteism, the caste system and caste-based discriminations. March 8 becomes the occasion for a charter of demands which reflect the struggle for women's emancipation from class, caste and sex-based inequalities and oppressions.

This book is therefore extremely timely and am sure will be of lasting interest to the generation of young women who are joining the ranks of the movements for women's emancipation with the dream of building a more equitable and just society.

I once again take this opportunity to congratulate the author for his contribution to the struggle through this important publication.

Brinda Karat
Polit Bureau Member, Communist Party of India (Marxist) and former General Secretary of All India Democratic Women's Association

Foreword

In recent years, the International Women's Day has become popular in India, owing in many ways to the attention given to it by the media and advertising industry. Notwithstanding the emergent interest, its origins, both globally and in India, go back to almost a century and in an ironic contrast to the zeal of corporate advertisers, deeply immersed in a socialist historical context.

As growing numbers of young, ebullient women and men now join the women's movement, it is important that they are familiar with and draw upon its rich histories, both in India and worldwide. To this end the book by Comrade R. Jawahar makes an invaluable contribution and I hope it will be read and appreciated widely.

This book traces the origin of International Women's Day to the Socialist Women's International Conference in 1910. It traces the origin of 'March 8' to the Russian revolution begun by women workers on March 8, 1917. It shows how the International Women's Day has come to be celebrated on March 8 permanently according to the decision of Communist Women's International in 1921. It also covers the important events that took place after 1921 regarding International Women's Day.

The equally important appendix of the book *Myths vs Reality* clarifies many widespread myths related to International Women's Day and the date March 8.

Comrade Jawahar has done all this with painstaking and meticulous research authenticating all the important points with documents.

Today when in India we find the massive rise of fascist tendencies and systematic curtailment of dissent, March 8 assumes far greater significance. Like the radical women's movement of the early 1940s in India, which rallied against fascism, we need to connect the women's struggle for equality with the overall struggle for true democracy and secularism.

I hope through this book on March 8 International Women's Day, this message reaches the women at the grassroots.

I take this opportunity not only to congratulate but to thank Comrade R. Jawahar for his efforts to popularize the idea behind the globally observed women's festival, the International Women's Day.

Annie Raja

National Executive Committee Member, Communist Party of India and General Secretary, National Federation of Indian Women (NFIW)

Foreword

International Women's Day is a celebration of more than a century of women's mass movements demanding equality and freedom.

It is important to remember that it was the socialist revolutionary women who began observing International Women's Day demanding the right to vote and an 8-hour working day. Those working class women and revolutionary socialists struggled for women's freedom – and for a revolution that would free not only women but the world's people from oppressive shackles.

It is also important to remember that March 8 has been made as the permanent date for International Women's Day to commemorate the Russian Revolution begun by women workers on March 8, 1917.

This is a history that the market and most of our ruling politicians would like us to forget, as they seek to appropriate International Women's Day (IWD) and empty it of its true historical and contemporary significance.

It is here that the importance of this excellent book by Comrade Jawahar is felt. Comrade Jawahar lays before us the history of International Women's Day—in particular the role of working class women, and Communist women, in bringing International Women's Day into being. With painstaking research and yet in a lucid and readable way that even a child can enjoy, he introduces the reader to this lively chapter of history.

The history of the Communist and working class women who laid the foundations of International Women's Day can then remind us of the need for the women's movement and Left movement to fight capitalism and patriarchy as a single system. Women's liberation is necessary for people's liberation, and people's liberation is necessary for women's liberation.

I hope that many will read, enjoy and share Comrade Jawahar's book. It is a book, not for bookshelves but for factories, fields, street meetings, schools, colleges and universities. It is a book that can be translated into many Indian languages and rendered into audio-visual formats as well.

Long live the legacy of International Women's Day! Naari Mukti Sabki Mukti! Women's Liberation, Everyone's Liberation!

Kavita Krishnan

Polit Bureau Member, Communist Party of India (Marxist-Leninist) (Liberation) and National Secretary, All India Progressive Women's Association

In Lieu of Acknowledgement

What is Communism, asked some young women in the 1990s. What is Marxism? What is Feminism? I did my best to answer their questions. They joined the Communist parties. They got to work building these ideas. A few years ago, some of these women and girls asked, "Why are there different versions of the origin and establishment of International Women's Day?" I did not know the answer to their question. Cursory investigation led nowhere. I had to research the question more thoroughly. It has been a thrilling journey, which has taken me two years. This book is the product of that research.

When I pursued the references of many articles online, it led me to websites in French, German, Russian, Portuguese, Finnish and other languages which I don't know! With the help of Google Translate, I have been able to understand the essence of the matter.

There are many myths, factual errors, unsubstantiated statements, lapses in memory of the initiators of International Women's Day themselves and so on which are more popular than the reality itself! I have tried my best to set things right in this book.

I want to thank Prof. Choi Chatterjee for her book *Celebrating Women: Gender, Festival Culture, and Bolshevik Ideology, 1910-1939*, Pittsburg, University of Pittsburg Press, 2002, from which I have benefited immensely regarding the women's role in the Russian Revolution.

The first person I want to thank, who helped me directly, is comrade **Renée Côté**.

I have dedicated this book to her along with two other comrades. She has been kind enough to respond to all my e-mails which were not a few! She has typed some of her mails at around 3 am at her home in the US, after finishing her busy schedule! Renée e-mailed a copy of the page from her book which contains one of the most important documents. She also got this German document translated into English by her friend Marianne for me.

Then she sent her French book on International Women's Day and her English book *Was My Mother Schizophrenic?* Renée continued to discuss with me and to encourage me in spite of many serious differences of opinion between us.

Thank you, dear comrade Renée!

I am grateful to:

Comrade Brinda Karat, Polit Bureau Member, Communist Party of India (Marxist), and former General Secretary of the All India Democratic Women's Association,

Comrade Annie Raja, National Executive Committee Member, Communist Party of India and General Secretary, National Federation of Indian Women, Comrade Kavita Krishnan, Polit Bureau member, Communist Party of India (Marxist-Leninist) (Liberation) and National Secretary,

All India Progressive Women's Association for their kind Forewords to this book.

My warmest appreciation to comrade G. Ramakrishnan, Polit Bureau member and Tamil Nadu State Secretary, Communist Party of India (Marxist). When my series of articles on International Women's Day was published in *Nakkheeran,* Tamil magazine, he regularly read it and encouraged me. He advised me to expand it with more details and publish it in English and Tamil. He assured me of all help needed and kept his word in deed although he has been very busy with the party work.

Thank you, dear comrade G.R.!

My thanks to my dear friend and comrade A.K. Padmanabhan, Polit Bureau member, Communist Party of India (Marxist) for his help. With much effort he got, the pdf file of the book *Legacy of International Women's Day* written by comrade Hemalata and promptly e-mailed it to me. He has shown a keen interest in my work and encouraged me.

I am grateful to comrade C. Mahendiran, National Council member, Communist Party of India for his kind help.

My thanks to comrade S. Balasundaram, Central Committee member, Communist Party of India (Marxist-Leninist) (Liberation) for his interest in this book and help.

Nakkheeran Gopal, Editor, *Nakkheeran,* Tamil magazine, published twice a week, deserves more than thanks. He published my series of articles on International Women's Day which is the synopsis of this book. He has already published many of my articles and the book *Communism: Naetru, Indru, Naalai* in Tamil. Not only that. He is like my brother who has been helping me in many ways.

I thank Kamaraj warmly. When he was the Associate Editor of *Nakkheeran* he was instrumental in publishing the said articles. He was kind enough to tolerate all the trouble I gave him! He is also like my brother.

My thanks to comrade Professor Vijay Prashad for his suggestions regarding editing as well as improving my English. This book has benefited greatly from many of his suggestions.

I cannot but thank my friend T.S. Subramanian, Senior Associate Editor, *Frontline,* my son Darwin, Film Director, for their help and my friend P. Vedarajan for his nice cover design of this book.

I don't know how to thank my wife C. Pooranam, former Professor of Economics, Queen Mary's College, Chennai, for her immeasurable help.

I thank Aakar Books for publishing this book.

July 4, 2016 R. Jawahar

1
What is International Women's Day?

What is International Women's Day?

It is not what has become of it in contemporary India – a time to conduct cooking competitions for women or a time for discount sales of jewellery, saris and other commodities. Nor is it a time to thank women for their presence. This is the absurd co-optation of this day by capitalist social forces.

International Women's Day is a day to recall the struggles by women for rights and liberation, and to plan for future struggles. This day is the creature of working women and their representatives, who fought to transform society. International Women's Day is in honour of the working women who began the revolutionary process that included the first socialist revolution.

Eleanor Marx said in 1891,

> And the woman herself reduced to the very lowest verge of misery, of despair, and of dependence, earning a wage that—even in the more skilled kinds of labour—generally means starvation, having, in addition to the long hours of labour for the employer, to do work of the "domestic"

> sort for her more immediate task-master; or where she is a widow, or unmarried mother with children dependent upon her, or even when she is alone in the world, having to toil on long after men for the most part have ceased work ....[1]

Does not the same situation, in *essence,* exist even today? Then, what is the situation of women who do the domestic work alone? She is doing this vexatious work without a single holiday until her death.

Class domination and male chauvinism combine to produce the situation faced by women then and now. It is the heroic struggles of women that promise a new society in which all human beings could live with equality, love and happiness. It is those struggles that produced International Women's Day.

One of the struggles is to protect and develop the history and living heritage of International Women's Day. The myths that surround it are many. We shall explore these myths in the appendix of the book.

Before we go to the myths, let us understand the *real* origin and establishment of International Women's Day and the date March 8.

2
First International

Oh, roaring assemblies of machines,
Shall I tell your beginning and end?
Is it not true you were born
by the labour of our workers?

—Tamil poet Bharathidasan

Workers in factories from Manchester to Madras toiled without any time limit in the 1800s. They became machines themselves. Workers died young – the backbreaking and heartbreaking work was not endurable.

Such a young woman's story of 1863 moved Karl Marx greatly. He wrote about this in his book *Capital*:

> In the last week of June, 1863, all the London daily papers published a paragraph with the "sensational" heading, "Death from simple over-work." It dealt with the death of the milliner, Mary Anne Walkley, 20 years of age, employed in a highly respectable dressmaking establishment, exploited by a lady with the pleasant name of Elise.
>
> The old, often-told story was once more recounted. This girl worked, on an average, 16½ hours, during the season often 30 hours, without a break, while her failing labour-

power was revived by occasional supplies of sherry, port, or coffee. It was just now the height of the season. It was necessary to conjure up in the twinkling of an eye the gorgeous dresses for the noble ladies bidden to the ball in honour of the newly-imported Princess of Wales.

Mary Anne Walkley had worked without intermission for 26½ hours, with 60 other girls, 30 in one room that only afforded one-third of the cubic feet of air required for them. At night, they slept in pairs in one of the stifling holes into which the bedroom was divided by partitions of board. And this was one of the best millinery establishments in London. Mary Anne Walkley fell ill on the Friday, died on Sunday, without, to the astonishment of Madame Elise, having previously completed the work in hand.

The doctor, Mr. Keys, called too late to the death-bed, duly bore witness before the coroner's jury that 'Mary Anne Walkley had died from long hours of work in an over-crowded work-room, and a too small and badly ventilated bedroom.' In order to give the doctor a lesson in good manners, the coroner's jury thereupon brought in a verdict that 'the deceased had died of apoplexy, but there was reason to fear that her death had been accelerated by over-work in an over-crowded workroom.'

"Our white slaves," cried the *Morning Star*, the organ of the Free-traders, Cobden and Bright, "who are toiled into the grave, for the most part silently pine and die." [2]

But that silence did not last long. It built on older currents of workers' struggles on both sides of the Atlantic Ocean. New efforts sought to unite the workers on an international level.

In 1864, the representatives of workers of Great Britain, Germany, France, Poland and Italy met in London. A range of socialists and trade unionists came to this meeting. Among them was Karl Marx. Out of this meeting came the International Workingmen's Association, which would later be known as the First International.

Later, in the International's General Council meeting, Marx delivered the Inaugural Address, which set out the policy of the International. It was adopted unanimously.[3]

Marx pointed to the nature of industrial development – wealth on one side for the capitalists, poverty and starvation on the other for workers. The problem here was political, not natural.

Hence, Marx said,

> To conquer political power has, therefore, become the great duty of the working classes...... Proletarians of all countries, unite![4]

This call continued to echo in the subsequent conferences and congresses.

But side by side the contradictions and splits grew among the leaders with different schools of thought. And after about ten years the First International came to an end.

Marx said then with scientific prophesy,

> ".... instead of dying out, the International did only pass from its first period of incubation to a higher one where its already original tendencies have in part become realities. In the course of its progressive development, it will yet have to undergo many a change, before the last chapter of its history can be written."[5]

This prophesy came to be realized later.

Marx died in 1883.

Socialist parties and trade unions grew and spread. In this process thundered the historic May Day struggle!

3
Second International

1886, May 1.

The American workers started a general strike on this day and held massive rallies demanding 'eight hour work day.' The centre of the struggle was Chicago. In the following days many workers were killed in Chicago in police firing and many more arrested. Four were hanged the next year.

One of the four, August Spies, shouted,

> "The time will come when our silence will be more powerful than the voices you strangle today. " [6]

This historic struggle started on May 1. Hence it would become May Day in the lexicon of the workers' movement. More powerful movements followed.

The founding conference of Socialist International, also called Second International, was held at Paris in 1889 with the help of Frederick Engels. [7] Around 400 delegates, from Germany, France, USA, England, Russia and other countries participated in the congress. Almost all of them were Marxists including August Bebel, Clara Zetkin, Eleanor Marx and Georgi Plekhanov. [8]

(Here, a note about the usage of the word *'socialist'*. At that time the word *communist* did not come into usage widely. All activists of the Second or Socialist International were called socialists. Many of them including Lenin and Clara Zetkin began to call themselves communists later.)

> At the congress, Zetkin raised the issue of working women. She was critical of many socialists who opposed the entrance of women into industry and for blaming women for the lowering of wages and lengthening of the working day.
>
> She argued that working women, like working men, suffered under long working hours and extremely low wages. Because the fundamental interests of working women were identical with those of working men, it was clear that liberation for working class women could come by allying with working men under the banner of socialism.
>
> Although the speech generated tremendous applause, the congress passed a resolution calling for work for women to be forbidden "in all branches of industry where the work is particularly damaging to the female organism". Night work for women was to be forbidden as well.
>
> However, the congress also declared "that male workers have a duty to take women into their ranks upon a basis of equal rights, and demand in principle, equal pay for equal work for the workers of both sexes and without discrimination of nationality." [9]

Many resolutions regarding the unity of workers, unity of socialists and economic and political rights of workers were passed at the congress.

The Congress had the Chicago workers in mind. The famous resolution on May Day was also passed as follows:

> "The Congress decides to organize a great international demonstration, so that in all countries and in all cities on one appointed day the toiling masses shall demand of the state authorities the legal reduction of the working day to eight hours, as well as the carrying out of other decisions of the Paris Congress. Since a similar demonstration has already been decided upon for May 1, 1890, by the American Federation of Labour at its Convention in St. Louis, December, 1888, this day is accepted for the international demonstration. The workers of the various countries must organize this demonstration according to conditions prevailing in each country."[10]

From 1890, May Day has been celebrated across the world as International Workers' Day. Thus the first congress of the Socialist International created a new awakening among workers and socialists. Through this progress was born the international socialist women's movement.

4

International Socialist Women's Movement

The fourth congress of Socialist International was held in London in 1896. Socialist women delegates met separately for the first time there. They discussed the possibility of holding a Socialist Women's conference.

The seventh congress was held at Stuttgart, Germany, in 1907. Lenin also took part in it.

> *The first International Conference of Socialist Women* was held concurrently on August 17, 1907.[11]

In those times there was no universal suffrage in any big country including those which claimed themselves as democratic countries having an elected parliamentary system. Even in England, which is called by many the cradle of modern democracy, there was no universal suffrage; only men, that too propertied men, had the right to vote and to be elected. [12]

Therefore workers were demanding this right for all men. But the socialists, particularly women socialists, were demanding this right for all women as well. In this situation this demand was emphasized in the first International Conference of Socialist Women. But opposition came from some women delegates themselves.

About this, Lenin wrote later:

> Both at this Conference and in the Congress Commission there was an interesting dispute between the German and Austrian Social-Democrats on the draft resolution.
>
> In their campaign for universal suffrage the Austrians tended to play down the demand for equal rights of men and women; on practical grounds they placed the main emphasis on male suffrage.
>
> Clara Zetkin and other German Social-Democrats rightly pointed out to the Austrians that they were acting incorrectly, and that by failing to press the demand that the vote be granted to women as well as men, they were weakening the mass movement.
>
> The concluding words of the Stuttgart resolution ("the demand for universal suffrage should be put forward *simultaneously* for both men and women").....[13]

Then Zetkin was elected secretary of the International Women's Secretariat.[14] The magazine *Die Gleichheit* (Equality), of which Zetkin was the editor, was recognized as the official journal of the organization.[15]

Socialist women went from this conference to their countries, where they intensified their struggles.

5

The First Woman's Day at City Level and National Level

WOMAN'S DAY AT THE GARRICK

TWO of the most capable women speakers in the Socialist movement of America will address the Garrick audience next Sunday morning in the absence of Mr. Lewis, who is lecturing in the interest of the Daily Socialist. The men patrons of the Garrick meeting are urged to turn out in force. Women should need no inviting. Corrine S. Brown will preside.

Education of the Working Class

Woman and the Socialist Party

Ben Hanford of New York City will speak on "Chicago."

Some Matters of Importance

Appreciated in New York

Pledges on the Garrick fund not yet paid are now overdue and it is respectfully suggested they should be paid at the earliest convenience of the donors.

Chicago Daily Socialist, vendredi, 1er mai 1908

Chicago Daily Socialist dated May 1, 1908

In 1908 there were enthusiastic meetings in Chicago and New York for women's rights. Particularly the meeting held in Chicago at Garrick Theatre was a historic one.

The women's section of the Socialist Party of America successfully organized there a mass meeting as 'Woman's Day' on *May 3, 1908*.

This was the first Woman's Day held at city level.[16]

Inspired by these developments, the Socialist Party of America formed the 'National Woman's Committee ' the same year. This committee passed many resolutions including women's right to vote.[17]

Following this, the executive committee of the Socialist Party of America passed the following resolution:

> "We recommend to all locals (branches) of the socialist party to reserve the last Sunday in February 1909 for organizing a demonstration in support of women's right to vote."[18]

It was published in *Chicago Daily Socialist* dated December 28, 1908.

There were no words as 'Woman's Day' in the resolution or in the announcements of the demonstrations or the meetings.[19]

Anyhow on *February 28, 1909,* successful 'Woman Suffrage Demonstration' and 'Woman Suffrage Meeting' were held in many places in America. Women and men participated in these movements massively. It was mentioned as 'Woman's Day' in the news published by the Socialist press.

> *Therefore this was the first Woman's Day held at national level.*[20]

Such events continued to be held in the USA on the last Sunday of February till 1913. [21]

> The historic conference, which decided to observe *'Women's Day' internationally,* was held next year, i.e. in 1910.

6

The Real Origin of International Women's Day

The congress of the Socialist International was held in Copenhagen, the capital of Denmark, from August 28 to September 3, 1910.

Concurrently, the *second International Socialist Women's Conference was held on August 26–27, 1910*. About 100 delegates from 17 countries participated. Clara Zetkin presided.

After elaborate discussions, many resolutions including those on women's right to vote, maternity insurance, protection of mother and child and against war were passed.[22]

With those resolutions the historic resolution was passed on 'Women's Day'.

frage, and they must raise this demand in their propaganda as well as in the Parliament, and insist on it with all their power. In countries where Manhood Suffrage is already far advanced or completely achieved, the Socialist Parties must take up the fight for the universal Woman's Suffrage, and with that naturally put forward all the demands which remain in order to obtain complete citizenship for the male proletariat.

It is the duty of the Socialist Women's movement in all countries to take part in all struggles which the Socialist Parties fight for the democratization of the Suffrage, and that with all possible energy; but also to see that in this fight the question of the universal Woman Suffrage is insisted on with due regard to its importance of principle and practice."

The Social-Democratic Women of Germany
and the Federation of the Social-Democratic Party's
organization of Berlin and neighborhood.

2. In order to forward political enfranchisement of women it is the duty of the Socialist women of all countries to agitate according to the above-named principles indefatigably among the laboring masses; enlighten them by discourses and literature about the social necessity and importance of the political emancipation of the female sex and use therefore every opportunity of doing so. For that propaganda they have to make the most especially of elections to all sorts of political and public bodies. In case the women have the right of voting at such bodies—local and provincial administrative bodies, arbitration-courts for trade disputes, state sickness insurance—the women must be urged to make full and reasonable use of their right; if the women have no vote at all, or a limited one, the socialist women must unite and guide them into the struggle for their right; in any case, there must be emphasized thoroughly the demand for full political Women Suffrage.

On occasion of the annual May demonstration—without regard to its form—the request of full political equality of the sexes must be proclaimed and substantiated. In agreement with the class-conscious political and trade organizations of the proletariat in their country the socialist women of all nationalities have to organize a special Women's Day, which in first line has to promote Women Suffrage propaganda. This demand must be discussed in connection with the whole women's question according to the socialist conception of social things. The conference must have an international character and be prepared with care.

Clara Zetkin, Kate Duncker and other comrades.

3. Considering that even in those countries in which the so-called universal suffrage exists, only one-half of the adult population enjoy it, but the women are disfranchised;

considering that only the action of the whole proletariat without any distinction of sex is creating a power strong enough to attain the ends pursued by the struggling and enlightened working class, and taking into account that the struggle for emancipation of the working women will be tremendously advanced, if we make the demand of political rights for women one of the most actual reforms we strive for;

The Second International Women's Conference resolves to urge all Socialist

The draft resolution proposed to the conference, published in 1910 in a booklet

The draft resolution was submitted in writing signed by "Clara Zetkin, Kate Dunker and other comrades".

The relevant portion of this draft resolution was,

> "On occasion of the annual May demonstration—without regard to its form—the request of full political equality of the sexes must be proclaimed and substantiated. In

> agreement with the class-conscious, political and trade organizations of the proletariat of their countries, the Socialist women of all nationalities have to organize a special Women's Day, which in first line has to promote Women Suffrage propaganda. This demand must be discussed in connection with the whole women's question according to the socialist conception of social things. The conference must have an international character and be prepared with care."[23]

The resolution did not propose *any specific date* for Women's Day. The delegates adopted the resolution unanimously, with great enthusiasm.[24]

> *This resolution of the second International Socialist Women's Conference in 1910 was the real origin of International Women's Day.*

The Socialist Women implemented the decision to celebrate Women's Day with fervour. They observed *the first International Women's Day* on Sunday, March 19, 1911 in Austria, Denmark, Germany and Switzerland.[25]

Why did the Socialists pick March 19? In 1920, Kollontai, an important Bolshevik leader, reflected back on the origins of International Women's Day.

She wrote,

> "This date was not chosen at random. Our German comrades picked the day because of its historic importance for the German proletariat. On the March 19, in the year of the 1848 revolution, the Prussian king recognized for the first time the strength of the armed people and gave way before the threat of a proletarian uprising. Among the many promises he made, which he later failed to keep, was the introduction of votes for women."[26]

Kollantai recorded the widespread triumph of the day,

> "The first International Women's Day took place in 1911. Its success succeeded all expectation. Germany and Austria on Working Women's Day was one seething, trembling sea of women. Meetings were organized everywhere—in the small towns and even in the villages halls were packed so full that they had to ask male workers to give up their places for the women.
>
> "This was certainly the first show of militancy by the working woman. Men stayed at home with their children for a change, and their wives, the captive housewives, went to meetings. During the largest street demonstrations, in which 30,000 were taking part, the police decided to remove the demonstrators' banners: the women workers made a stand. In the scuffle that followed, bloodshed was averted only with the help of the socialist deputies in Parliament." [26]

Next year, on Sunday, *May 12, 1912,* International Women's Day was celebrated in many countries including Germany[27] and Sweden.[28]

In Stuttgart (Germany) the famous Marxist revolutionary Rosa Luxemburg spoke at the International Women's Day rally. She proudly said:

> "More than a hundred and fifty thousand women are organized in unions ..... Many thousands of politically organized women have rallied to the banner of Social Democracy; the Social Democratic women's paper (*Die Gleichcheit,* edited by Clara Zetkin) has more than one hundred thousand subscribers..."[29]

The link between the proletarian women's struggles organized in unions and socialist parties as well as in the suffrage movement was strong.

Next year, on Sunday, *March 2, 1913,* International Women's Day was celebrated more vigorously.

Frauenwahlrecht!

Jener Tag.

Clara Zetkin published a special pamphlet dated March 2, 1913 on that day.

What was extraordinary this year was that the International Women's Day was celebrated in Russia for the first time.

7

International Women's Day in Russia

One who says 'hm' will be jailed.
One who asks 'why?' will be exiled.

—wrote Tamil poet Bharathi about Russia under the rule of the Tsar. Such was the oppressive condition in Russia then.

The Communist Party under the leadership of Lenin was almost functioning underground. Although the name of this party at that time was Russian Social–Democratic Labour Party (Bolsheviks), it was generally referred to as the *Bolshevik Party*.[30] We will also refer to it as the Bolshevik Party.

In the oppressive situation under the Tsar's rule, the Party decided to celebrate International Women's Day on Sunday *March 2, 1913* (according to the old style Julian Calendar which was followed in Russia then, on February 17, 1913).

> Elaborate preparations were made for a few months before the Day in some cities including St Petersburg, the capital of Russia, at that time.

The St Petersburg committee of the Party organized an International Women's Day holiday commission led by

Samoilova and Kudelli including two factory workers Shura Alekseeva and Nikiferova. Many articles were published in *Pravda* (Truth), the party paper, in connection with International Women's Day and women's rights.

In a *Pravda* article it was said, "Our women for the first time today will enter the general family of the proletarian movement, and for the first time, will feel the strong ties that bind her, not only to the women workers of different countries, but to the working class in general."

Many tactics were adopted to get police permission for the meeting. The women published a false date for the event (which had been planned for a week later) and asked for permission to hold a "Scientific Morning" to debate the woman question. The meeting was eventually held on March 2 at the Great Hall of the Kalashnikov Exchange on Kharkhov Street. Thousands of women gathered at the hall, as women outside handed out red carnations to raise funds for prisoners and those in exile.

At the event, Shura Alekseeva, a textile worker, spoke about the life of working women. She had been assisted by Anna Ulyanova, Lenin's elder sister, who was a member of the Bolshevik Party and by Samoilova to prepare the speech. In her memoirs, Alekseeva wrote,

> "Never before had I spoken in front of such a large audience and naturally, like any novice orator, was confused. The policemen in the front row were directly in front of me. They moved, scraped their chairs, talked and laughed .... I suddenly realized that I could not remember a single word or idea from the précis. Looking at the notebook, the letters seemed to swim and I could not understand or remember a single thing. I stood there. And then literally, someone pushed me. I laid aside the

notebook and began to speak of the life of the female textile worker.

As a textile worker, Alekseeva had plenty of first-hand experience and spoke fluently and movingly of the terrible conditions of labour in the factories, of over work, of meagre payment, of sexual harassment, of being forced to sleep with the superiors .... Women workers from the audience murmured approvingly, moved about and even rose from their seats agitatedly.

She also spoke about prostitution and the dire need that drove women to this dishonouring trade. She said that Socialist women were transferring gender relations of a capitalist society to the future proletarian community and called for all women to join the proletarian family and march hand in hand towards a bright future.

The speech was loudly applauded. But Alekseeva was so convinced that she had ruined her presentation that as soon as she walked off the stage, she burst into tears! Samoilova was very amused by her reaction and tried to comfort her by praising her performance.

But certainly the watching police officers had realized the revolutionary import of her speech since she was arrested the same night.

(International Women's Day events in Russia in 1913, 1914 and 1917 are described here based on the book by Choi Chatterjee)[31]

The first International Women's Day in St. Petersburg and elsewhere had been a tremendous success. Anna Ulyanova recalled that women now joined unions, clubs and illegal organizations. The St. Petersburg police agreed. International Women's Day was not "celebrated very widely," wrote the intelligence officer, "but it served towards awakening the solidarity of women workers and their interest in political party work...Women have been elected as members of the committees of various cultural-educational organizations and professional unions."

8

In Spite of Arrests and Repression ...

International Women's Day of 1914 came as the war drums beat across Europe. On March 8, women from Russia to Germany celebrated the day with apprehension. The First World War was on the horizon. The Bolshevik Party prepared carefully for the Day. The police refused to grant permission for the celebration. Eventually they allowed one meeting to be held in St. Petersburg.

Bolshevik women tried to publish the first issue of *Rabotnitsa* (Woman Worker) on March 8. The editorial board gathered for a last-minute meeting at Praskovia Kudelli's tiny apartment on March 3. Everyone was in a cheerful frame of mind. The discussions on the periodical were enthusiastic.

Suddenly the door flew open and several police officers burst in. They arrested all four of these key comrades. The next night, on March 4, the police arrested thirteen other members of the International Women's Day Holiday Commission. The police then went after others, arresting more than thirty of the organizers.

Who was going to finish *Rabotnitsa* and prepare for the Day? One comrade, Anna Elizarova—Lenin's sister—had been late for the meeting on March 3. She escaped arrest.

Anna Elizarova and other comrades finished the paper and distributed twelve thousand copies on International Women's Day.

The state deployed thousands of police to disrupt the Day. The police closed down the one permitted event, which sent workers onto the streets—singing revolutionary songs. The police used whips to flog participants, arresting many. Those in prison continued their celebration there. Women met in scattered groups across the city to celebrate the Day. They bought *Rabotnitsa* and read it aloud on the streets. The Bolsheviks organized working-class men to join the women to make this an all-proletarian event. Late at night, three hundred workers gathered at Troitskii Bridge, shouting, "We greet Women's Day." The police dispersed them. Their jubilation would be short-lived—World War I broke out four months later.

9

"Turn the Weapons"

Sixteen million people died in the Great War, which went on for four years.[32] The Socialist International was a casualty of the war—despite having taken positions against chauvinism and war, many of the socialist leaders became *'patriots'*, namely bourgeois jingoists, i.e. capitalist chauvinist patriots.

Lenin wrote bitterly against the treachery of these socialist leaders. On November 1, 1914, Lenin wrote—on behalf of the Bolsheviks,

> "..... Seizure of territory and subjugation of other nations, the ruining of competing nations and the plunder of their wealth, distracting the attention of the working masses from the internal political crises in Russia, Germany, Britain and other countries, disuniting and nationalist stultification of the workers, and the extermination of their vanguard so as to weaken the revolutionary movement of the proletariat—these comprise the sole actual content, importance and significance of the present war.......
>
> "The opportunists have wrecked the decisions of the Stuttgart, Copenhagen and Basle congresses, which made it binding on socialists of all countries to combat chauvinism in all and any conditions, made it binding on

> socialists to reply to any war begun by the bourgeoisie and governments, with intensified propaganda of civil war and social revolution. ......
>
> "The greater the sacrifices imposed by the war the clearer will it become to the mass of the workers that the opportunists have betrayed the workers' cause and that the weapons must be turned against the government and the bourgeoisie of each country.....
>
> "It is only along this path that the proletariat will be able to shake off its dependence on the chauvinist bourgeoisie, and, in one form or another and more or less rapidly, take decisive steps towards genuine freedom for the nations and towards socialism."[33]

Revolutionary socialist women did not have their hands tied. On the suggestion of Inessa Armand, one of the Bolshevik woman leaders, Clara Zetkin convened the Socialist Women's International Conference on March 26-28, 1915 at Bern, Switzerland, a neutral country.

Around 30 delegates managed to attend the conference in those difficult times from eight countries including Clara Zetkin, Krupskaya (one of the Bolshevik woman leaders and Lenin's wife) and Inessa.[34]

After passing many resolutions, a manifesto—*To the Women of the Proletariat*—was released at the end of the conference. It asked "Where are your husbands? Where are your sons?" It said "the workers have nothing to gain from this war, they have everything to lose, everything, everything that is dear to them" and called on women to act, to demand peace.[35]

The pacifist tone did not please the Bolsheviks, who wanted to go further.[36] Anyhow Clara Zetkin and the French delegate Simonaue were imprisoned after their return to their countries on treason charges.[37, 38]

Earlier on Sunday, March 7, 1915, International Women's Day was also celebrated in Switzerland.[38]

The war devastated Russia. Almost two million soldiers died, with an equal number as prisoners of war and a million missing.[39] Poverty stalked the land. Workers in Russia saw their conditions deteriorate. Protests became commonplace.

> Revolutionary women played an exemplary role. By 1917, in the capital city Petrograd (old name St Petersburg) alone, eight hundred and eighty-nine women went to jail as political prisoners.

10

The Real Origin of the 'March 8'

The revolutionary march of working women in Petrograd in March, 1917

No more tears! No more silence! The working women of Petrograd and suburbs burst into action!

That was *1917, March 8* (according to the old style Julian calendar which was followed in Russia then, it was February 23), International Women's Day in Russia.

The workers of textile factories of Vyborg region, all of them women almost, went on strike and came to the streets.

You could have noted that hitherto, the International Women's Day had been observed on a Sunday in all countries. Now for the first time on Thursday, a working day, March 8, 1917, the Petrograd women workers observed it by striking work and rallying on streets.

They marched towards Nevskii Prospekt, the city's main thoroughfare, calling the workers to join them. At the metal factories, they threw snowballs and metal bits at the factory's windows—asking the men to come out, strike and raise their voices for bread and an end to the war. Younger workers started the flood. Seven thousand five hundred workers poured out of the factories. When the women saw them coming, they wildly cheered and then holding the workers by their hand, dragged them towards the main road.

Women from a cigarette factory burst into one metal works plant. One of their leaders, with a red band on her chest, loudly announced, "Comrades! Enough discussion! Come into the streets and we will ask for bread and freedom!". The workers joined them. Women who stood in long queues at food stores joined the march, some with their children. Students and office workers joined in.

At many places there were scuffles with the police. Women themselves tackled them either through persuasion or through force, chasing the police away. They also requested the soldiers to support them. One hundred and twenty-eight thousand people marched that day.[40] They carried signs that said, *Give Bread to Our Children, We, the Wives of Soldiers, Demand: End the War, Long Live Unity.* One more appeared—*Overthrow the Monarchy.*

This Russian Revolution began in these streets on March 8, 1917. In the history of Russia it is called 'February Revolution' because this March 8 was February 23, according to the old style Julian calendar which was followed in Russia then.

> *In this crucible of the Russian Revolution—International Women's Day's March 8 date has its real origin.*

11
The Fall of Monarchy

On the second day two hundred thousand people marched on the streets.[40]

The Bolsheviks had to shut down the transportation system as part of the General Strike. Nina Agadzhanova, a Bolshevik from the Caucasus region and part of the *Rabotnitsa* team, went on the streets. She stood between the rails of a tram car and forced herself to keep her place, although it showed no sign of slowing down. But the tram did come to a halt right in front of her. She felt terrible for a few moments but soon recovered her nerve. Climbing into the cab, Agadzhanova seized the keys from the driver. It was acts such as this that paralyzed Russia and pushed the revolution forward. By March 10, Petrograd was closed down.

In the evening, the Tsar telegraphed the commander of the Petrograd military district, "I order the disturbances to be stopped in the capital tomorrow." [41]

The military arrested hundreds of leaders—men and women. The army fired on protesters, killing one hundred and sixty nine people, wounding over a thousand. Outraged by this cruelty, section after section of the army began to join the people. The policemen who tried to stop them were arrested by them. Three fourths of the army in the city—sixty-six thousand soldiers—joined the revolution with their guns. Militant workers now had arms in hand. The historic 'Petrograd Soviet of Workers' and Soldiers' Deputies' was formed and by March 16 the Tsar abdicated.[42,43]

From the International Women's Day to the Revolution—that is the trajectory of the events.

12

The First Socialist Revolution of the World

Lenin speaks among revolutionaries during the socialist revolution (1917)

Autocracy was defeated, but the new government—led by bourgeois forces—failed the people. It was declared as one of the guiding principles of the provisional government that it would make "immediate arrangements for the calling of the Constituent Assembly on the basis of universal, equal and direct suffrage and secret ballot, which will determine the form of government and the constitution of the country." [44] But apart from this, it did not address the pressing questions of war, food, and land.

Lenin arrived in Russia in April, and released his April Theses to address this failure. He wrote,

> In our attitude towards the war, which under the new [provisional] government ..... unquestionably remains on Russia's part a predatory imperialist war owing to the capitalist nature of that government.....
>
> No support for the Provisional Government, the utter falsity of all its promises should be made clear, particularly of those relating to the renunciation of annexations.....
>
> Not a parliamentary republic—to return to a parliamentary republic from the Soviets of Workers' Deputies would be a retrograde step—but a republic of Soviets of Workers', Agricultural Labourers' and Peasants' Deputies throughout the country, from top to bottom.....
>
> ...... without the Soviets of Workers' and Soldiers' Deputies the convocation of the Constituent Assembly is not guaranteed and its success is impossible ...... [45]

Lenin's slogan—*All power to the Soviets*—resonated with the workers. The Soviets, however, wanted to give the bourgeois government a chance. But a leaked note from the new government to the Tsar's allies said that the government would "stand by its obligation towards our allies." They did not want to end the war.

This prompted armed demonstrations by furious soldiers in the streets against the government. In the meantime food deficit and prices went up. The toiling peasants began to seize the lands of big landlords. The government tried to suppress the agitations. Angered by these developments, the workers went on a general strike throughout the country. More than 500,000 workers and soldiers demonstrated in Petrograd.

The government spoke the language of the Tsar. The army men brought from the war front fired on the demonstrators. About four hundred people were killed and wounded. The agitation paused. The Petrograd Soviet admitted that the Bolsheviks had been correct.[46] The Russian Revolution's radical phase dawned.

The first socialist revolution of the world began. The Red Guards (workers' militia), soldiers and sailors seized important government institutions on November 7, 1917. On the next day, Lenin announced that the workers and peasants had assumed power.[47]

The triumphant march of socialist Russia began.

13

Unprecedented Achievements in Women's Rights

In the early morning of the same day, November 8, the first Decree (Act) on ending the war[48], the second decree on land to the cultivators without distinction of sex[49] and a resolution on forming the government of workers and peasants under the Chairmanship of Lenin [50] were adopted by the congress of soviets. Women entered positions of responsibility over the affairs of the state—Kollontai, for example, was Minister of Public Affairs[51]. Within the next three days, on November 11, a decree established eight-hour working day and a weekly holiday.[52]

Bharathi, the Tamil poet, welcomed these developments on November 17, 1917. He wrote "What is practised in Russia today under the leadership of Mr. Lenin ... is communism. When this ideology succeeds worldwide, the true civilization will succeed."

Within a year, many laws including the Constitution were promulgated in Russia, for the rights of toiling people, including and specifically for the rights of women, *for the first time in the world.*

The Constitution that the Soviet Government wrote was alert to the importance of women's liberation. Article 64 noted, "The right to vote and to be elected to the soviets is enjoyed by the ... citizens of both sexes, irrespective of religion, nationality, domicile, etc., of the Russian Socialist Federated Soviet Republic, who shall have completed their eighteenth year by the day of election."[53] Thus Russia became the first big country to give this right to women even before England and the USA.

By various Acts and orders, the Soviet decreed the following[54,55,56]:

- Equal pay for equal work and equal right to work without discrimination of sex.
- For pregnant women, eight weeks of paid holiday before child birth and eight weeks of paid holiday after child birth, at least half an hour break for every three hours to feed their baby, exemption from night work and over-time work, free prenatal and postnatal care along with cash allowances.
- Abolition of the power of church on registration of marriage and sanction of divorce. Marriage, registered by the government Registrar would only be valid. The Court would be the only authority for sanction of divorce. Making divorce law easy.
- Elimination of the distinction between "legitimate" and "illegitimate" children, using instead the carefully considered wording "children of parents who are not in a registered marriage." Thus, women could claim child support from men to whom they were not married.
- Establishment of the right of all children to parental support until the age of 18.

- Abortion made legal and free and safe medical help for it guaranteed.
- Homosexual acts and other consensual sexual activities were decriminalized.
- The principle that "the absolute non-interference of the state and society into sexual matters, so long as nobody is injured, and no one's interests are encroached upon" declared.

In 1919, Lenin wrote of the Soviet's record on women's liberation,

> Take the position of women. In this field, not a single democratic party in the world, not even in the most advanced bourgeois republic, has done in decades so much as a hundredth part of what we did in our very first year in power. We really razed to the ground the infamous laws placing women in a position of inequality, restricting divorce and surrounding it with disgusting formalities, denying recognition to children born out of wedlock, enforcing a search for their fathers, etc., laws numerous survivals of which, to the shame of the bourgeoisie and of capitalism, are to be found in all civilized countries. We have a thousand times the right to be proud of what we have done in this field.

Lenin did not, however, feel that enough had been done and hence he said,

> But the more thoroughly we have cleared the ground of the lumber of the old, bourgeois laws and institutions, the clearer it is to us that we have only cleared the ground to build on but are not yet building.

> Notwithstanding all the laws emancipating woman, she continues to be a domestic slave.
>
> The real emancipation of women, real communism, will begin only where and when an all-out struggle begins (led by the proletariat wielding the state power) against this petty housekeeping, or rather when its wholesale transformation into a large-scale socialist economy begins.
>
> Do we in practice pay sufficient attention to this question, which in theory every Communist considers indisputable? Of course not. Do we take proper care of the shoots of communism which already exist in this sphere? Again the answer is no.
>
> There is no doubt that we have far more organising talent among the working and peasant women than we are aware of, that we have far more people than we know of who can organize practical work, with the co-operation of large numbers of workers and of still larger numbers of consumers, without that abundance of talk, fuss, squabbling and chatter about plans, systems, etc., with which our big-headed "intellectuals" or half-baked "Communists" are "affected". But we do not nurse these shoots of the new as we should.[57]

By 1920, March 8 was declared a general holiday. Kollontai explained the importance of the day,

> On 1917, on this day, the great February revolution broke out. It was the working women of Petersburg who began this revolution; it was they who first decided to raise the banner of opposition to the Tsar and his associates. And so, working women's day is a double celebration for us...

> In the Soviet republic the working women and peasants don't need to fight for the franchise and for civil rights. They have already won these rights. The Russian workers and the peasant women are equal citizens—in their hands is a powerful weapon to make the struggle for a better life easier—the right to vote, to take part in the Soviets and in all collective organizations. But rights alone are not enough. We have to learn to make use of them. The right to vote is a weapon which we have to learn to master for our own benefit, and for the good of the workers' republic.
>
> In the two years of Soviet power, life itself has not been absolutely changed. We are only in the process of struggling for communism and we are surrounded by the world we have inherited from the dark and repressive past. The shackles of the family, of housework, of prostitution still weigh heavily on the working woman. Working women and peasant women can only rid themselves of this situation and achieve equality in life itself, and not just in law, if they put all their energies into making Russia a truly communist society.[58]

The dynamic of Soviet Russia spread across the world.

14

The Real Event that Established 'March 8'

The Second Conference of Communist Women's International. (In the first row from right) Kollontai, Clara Zetkin and others. (1921)

You can remember that Socialist International, also called Second International, split after the outbreak of World

War I and then the Russian socialist revolution succeeded under the leadership of the Bolshevik Party guided by Lenin in 1917.

The official name of the party at that time was Russian Social-Democratic Labour Party (Bolsheviks). It was changed to *'Russian Communist Party (Bolsheviks)'* officially in 1918.[59]

In the same year Moscow became the capital of Russia.[60]

Then the communists and the left socialists who supported the Russian Communist Party (Bolsheviks), started separate parties in the name of the Communist Party or with any other name in their countries.

Confederating these parties was formed the Communist International, Comintern in short, also called the Third International in 1919.[61] The second congress of Comintern was held in Petrograd and it continued and came to a close in Moscow in 1920.[62]

Inessa Armand assumed the leadership to hold the first Communist Women's International Conference in Moscow—concurrent with this Comintern meeting. The conference had vibrant discussions on many issues, but before it could be properly established after the conclusion of the conference, Inessa Armand died at the age of 46.[63] Zetkin was elected secretary of the International Women's Secretariat of the Comintern.[64]

On June 9–15, 1921, the second International Conference of Communist Women was held in Moscow. At this meeting, the delegates established 'March 8' as the permanent date for International Women's Day.

The Communist Women's International's official journal, *Die Kommunistische Fraueninternationale* (*The Communist*

Women's International), in its January-February 1922 issue wrote,

> Exhilaration welcomed the proposal of our Bulgarian women comrades, as well as the decision of the Second International Conference of Communist Women at Moscow, to observe the International Women's Day on March 8, the same day that the Russian comrades celebrate it. With joyous elation, the determined and daring resolve came into being. It brought the stunning memory of the giant demonstrations of the Petersburg women proletarians on March 8, 1917 for Peace and Freedom that had led to the Russian Revolution.....[65]

Before 1917, International Women's Day was celebrated on Sundays. From 1917, it was celebrated in Russia alone on the fixed date March 8. The Germans did not follow this but celebrated in 1920 on May 9[66], in 1921 on April 3[67], both Sundays.

After the 1921 Communist Women's International Conference's decision—on the proposals of the Bulgarians-International Women's Day on March 8 was a regular feature in the international communist calendar.

> *Therefore the real event that established 'March 8' as the permanent date for 'International Women's Day' was the decision of the Communist Women's International Conference in 1921.*

It is known that the centenary of the decision of the Socialist Women's International to observe 'Women's Day' was celebrated throughout the world including in India in 2010.

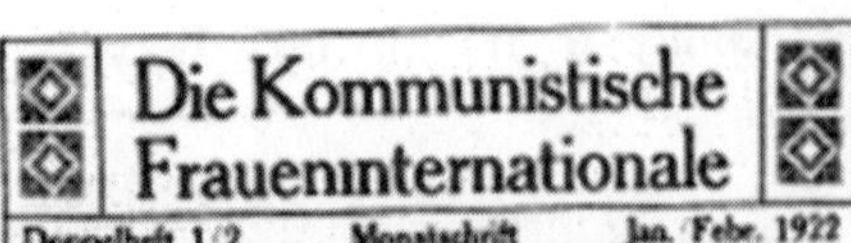

Die Kommunistische Fraueninternationale

Doppelheft 1/2 Monatschrift Jan. Febr. 1922

Der Internationale Kommunistische Frauentag.

Begeisterungsstürme begrüßten den Antrag unserer bulgarischen Genossinnen und den Beschluß der Zweiten Internationalen Konferenz der Kommunistinnen zu Moskau, den Internationalen Frauentag einheitlich am 8. März abzuhalten, an dem die russischen Genossinnen ihn begehen. Hoch schlugen die Herzen, weithin flog der Blick, und der Wille reckte sich hoch, kühn empor. Die Erinnerung flammte hinreißend auf, daß es die Riesendemonstration der Petersburger Proletarierinnen für Frieden und Freiheit gewesen, die am 8. März 1917 die russische Revolution eingeleitet hat.

The relevant page of *Die Kommunistische Fraueninternationale*

Likewise, it would be proper to celebrate the centenary of the decision of the Communist Women's International to observe International Women's Day on 'March 8' permanently, on June 9–15, 2021.

And, two more factors made International Women's Day to be observed as widely as it is being done today. One: the storm of feminism in the 1960s and 70s. Two: United Nations. Now we will go into these two factors.

15

The Storm of Feminism

After the decision of the Communist Women's International, communist women and supporters began to observe International Women's Day on March 8 uniformly from 1922.[68] But the socialists and others continued to observe it on different dates.[69]

At the end of and after the Second World War, Communist Parties came to power in many countries. These socialist states also celebrated International Women's Day on March 8 which stabilized March 8 further.[70] However, over time, International Women's Day began to be observed by fewer and fewer people other than communists.

In this situation the feminist movement appeared like a storm in America and Europe in the 1960s.

> What is feminism?
>
> Men and women are equals. There is no difference between them except the biological differences. They have equal rights and duties in all fields including political, economic, social and cultural fields, domestic work and child care. All kinds of domination including male chauvinism should be resisted and abolished. The ideology which insists on these and related stands can be called feminism generally.

The voices for women's rights have been raised for a long time. Anyhow the modern movement for women's rights began in the 1800s. It started as the women's movement against the slavery system in the 1820s in the UK and in the 1830s in the USA.[71] Step by step, it evolved into a movement for equal rights and women's suffrage. At that time the word *feminism* was coined in France and it spread.[72]

In 1848, a "Woman's Rights Convention—A convention to discuss the social, civil, and religious condition and rights of women" was held in the USA which said in its Declaration "... all men *and women* are created equal ..." and raised many demands including the right to vote for women.[73]

Then the socialist women's movement began to function at the end of the 1800s and at the beginning of the 1900s.

While this movement fought for equal rights for women, it gave first priority to socialism, as Clara Zetkin said "..... only the revolutionary overthrow of bourgeois society and the realization of socialism by the proletariat, in the struggle for emancipation, could bring the whole of womankind to a fully blooming and self-asserting humanity transcending formal statutory equality of both the sexes." [74]

We have already seen the development and achievements of the socialist and communist women's movement.

All these movements are called the first wave of feminism.

The second wave of feminism began in the 1960s in America.

On *November 1, 1961,* around 50,000 women went on strike and demonstrated throughout the US protesting against nuclear weapons and the US' war on Viet Nam. This agitation was organized by 'Women Strike for Peace'.

Then a number of organizations for civil and women's rights were formed.

The National Organization for Women was founded in 1966 and it said "We, men and women ..... believe that the time has come ..... to confront, with concrete action, the conditions that now prevent women from enjoying the equality of opportunity and freedom of choice which is their right, as individual Americans, and as human beings."

New York Radical Women was founded in 1967.

> "On September 7, 1968, NYRW protested the Miss America Pageant in Atlantic City, New Jersey. Hundreds of women marched on the Atlantic City Boardwalk with signs that criticized the pageant and called it a "cattle auction." During the live telecast, the women displayed from the balcony a banner that said "Women's Liberation."

Although this event is often considered to be where "bra-burning" took place, their actual symbolic protest consisted of placing bras, girdles, *Playboy* magazines, mops, and other evidence of the oppression of women into a trash can, but not lighting the objects on fire.

"NYRW said the pageant not only judged women based on ludicrous beauty standards but supported the immoral Vietnam War by sending the winner to entertain the troops. They also protested the racism of the pageant which had never yet crowned a black Miss America."[75]

> "Where else could one find such a perfect combination of American values—racism, militarism, capitalism—all

> packaged in one 'ideal' symbol, a woman?" asked Robin Morgan, one of the founders of NYRW.[76]

Chicago Women's Liberation Union was founded in 1969.

Vivian Rothstein, one of its founders, had travelled to North Viet Nam in 1967 at the height of the war to see for herself the extent of the destruction. Her experiences with the women's organizations in Viet Nam inspired her to emulate their example in the US. Therefore she along with others founded the CWLU.[77]

The principles of the organization were: "The struggle for women's liberation is a revolutionary struggle. Women's liberation is essential to the liberation of all oppressed peoples. Women's liberation will not be achieved until all people are free. We will struggle for the liberation of women and against male supremacy in all sections of society. We will struggle against racism, imperialism, and capitalism and dedicate ourselves to developing consciousness of their effects on women. We are dedicated to a democratic organization and understand a way to ensure democracy is through full exchange of information and ideas, full political debate and through the unity of theory and practice."[78]

Earlier, the journal *Voice of the Women's Liberation Movement,* dated March 1968 reported:

> International Women's Day was celebrated (on) March 8 by the Chicago chapters with a film, *Salt of the Earth* and an all-Movement party, the groups' first integrated function.[79]

Thus the women's liberation movement, also called feminist movement, spread out with a number of organizations, groups and movements and with different ideologies.

Some of them sharply criticized the communist and socialist parties too. Doris Wright, who became one of the founders of the National Black Feminist Organization[80], wrote in 1971:

> *Don't tell us about discrimination everywhere else; And don't tell us it comes only from class oppression. Look at yourselves.*
>
> *Don't tell us that "full freedom" can come only the "day after" the revolution. Our questions must be faced the day* before.
>
> *Furthermore, the words are not sufficient; Let's see, you* practise *it.*
>
> *..... You will have to learn that you are not the font of all wisdom—or of revolution......*[81]

Although there were many schools of thought such as this and others, the feminist movement in general helped to spread awareness on women's rights throughout the world and to get some legal rights for women.

And, it revived 'March 8: International Women's Day' among non-communist women widely which has been celebrated by communist women already.

In this situation the UN came forward, that too by the initiatives of communist women, to take some concrete measures on women's rights and for the celebration of International Women's Day officially.

16
The Role of Communist Women in the UN

In 1945, communist women joined together to create the Women's International Democratic Federation (WIDF)[82]. The Comintern had closed down by 1943,[83] as did the various Moscow-based international women's committees. WIDF emerged out of the need felt by communist women for an international secretariat to bring together democratic women's groups from all over the world.

In 1971, WIDF's Bureau at its meeting in Berlin stressed the importance of an international year for the advancement of women.[84] The next year, Freda Brown, President of the Union of Australian Women (affiliate of WIDF) and central committee member of the Communist Party of Australia,[85,86] sent a letter to the UN Secretary-General. Brown proposed that the UN hold an International Women's Year and prepare a Convention on the Elimination of All Forms of Discrimination against Women.[87]

At the March 1972 meeting of the UN Commission on the Status of Women, Hertta Kuusinen, a leader of the Communist Party of Finland and president of WIDF and who had observer status in the Commission, submitted the WIDF proposal for an International Women's Year. The proposal was backed by other NGO observers. Florica Andrei, representative of Romania, a socialist country, presented the proposal in her official capacity to the Commission. Helvi Sipilä, the Finnish government representative at that time and later the first woman Assistant Secretary-General of the UN, seconded the proposal. The Commission accepted the proposal. It sent it along to the General Assembly, who—in December 1972—proclaimed 1975 as the International Women's Year.

In 1975, the World Conference of the International Women's Year was held successfully in Mexico City. It was the first-ever global inter-governmental conference specifically organized to address women's issues and world problems from women's perspectives.

Helvi Sipilä later said,

> I cannot envisage that it could have taken place as early as 1975 without the untiring efforts of Hertta Kuusinen. She and [Shahnaz] Alami [an Iranian poet] who also represented the WIDF, worked very hard trying to persuade the regional groups, individual representatives of governments, members of the UN Secretariat and observers of non-governmental organizations of the need to have an International Women's Year as soon as possible.[88,89]

In anticipation of the Mexico City World Conference of the International Women's Year, on March 8, 1975 the UN celebrated International Women's Day for the first time.[90]

Two years later, in 1977, the UN General Assembly passed a resolution inviting all States to celebrate women's day.

Taking note of the report of the Secretary-General on the management of the Fund submitted to it at its thirty-second session,[189]

1. *Notes with satisfaction* the decisions taken by the Consultative Committee on the Voluntary Fund for the United Nations Decade for Women at its first two sessions, held in March and June 1977;[190]

2. *Expresses the hope* that the projects which the Consultative Committee has already approved will be implemented as soon as possible;

3. *Urges* the specialized agencies and other United Nations bodies concerned, including the United Nations Development Programme, to assist the regional commissions in formulating projects drawn up in connexion with the United Nations Decade for Women, with a view to submitting them to the Consultative Committee;

4. *Also urges* the specialized agencies and other United Nations bodies concerned, including the United Nations Development Programme, to co-operate closely with the Consultative Committee with a view to developing programmes which will contribute to the advancement of women;

5. *Requests* the Secretary-General to continue to submit annual reports on the management of the Fund and:

(*a*) To include in such reports a summary of the projects selected by the Consultative Committee for financing by the Fund;

(*b*) To submit periodically to the General Assembly progress reports on the execution of such projects.

105th plenary meeting
16 December 1977

32/142. Women's participation in the strengthening of international peace and security and in the struggle against colonialism, racism, racial discrimination, foreign aggression and occupation and all forms of foreign domination

The General Assembly,

Recalling its resolutions 3519 (XXX), 3520 (XXX) and 3521 (XXX) of 15 December 1975 and 31/136 of 16 December 1976,

Taking into account that secure peace and social progress, the establishment of the new international economic order as well as the full enjoyment of human rights and fundamental freedoms require the active participation of women, their equality and development,

Appreciating the contribution of women to the strengthening of international peace and security and to the struggle against colonialism, racism, racial discrimination, foreign aggression and occupation and all forms of foreign domination,

Emphasizing its grave concern that in some regions of the world colonialism, *apartheid*, racial discrimination and aggression continue to exist and territories are still occupied, which represents a most serious infringement of the principles of the Charter of the United Nations and of human rights of both women and men, and of the peoples' right to self-determination,

[189] A/32/174.
[190] *Ibid.*, sect. II.

Reaffirming the objectives of the United Nations Decade for Women, the Declaration of Mexico on the Equality of Women and Their Contribution to Development and Peace, 1975[191] and the World Plan of Action for the Implementation of the Objectives of the International Women's Year,[192]

1. *Takes note* of the report of the Secretary-General on the implementation of General Assembly resolution 3519 (XXX);[193]

2. *Calls upon* all States to continue to make their contribution to creating favourable conditions for the elimination of discrimination against women and for their full and equal participation in the social development process and to encourage broad participation of women in the effort to strengthen international peace, extend the process of international détente, curb the arms race and take measures for disarmament;

3. *Seizes the occasion* of the International Anti-*Apartheid* Year to be observed in 1978 to invite all States fully to support women exposed to colonialism, racism and *apartheid* in their just struggle against the racist régimes in southern Africa;

4. *Invites* all States to proclaim, in accordance with their historical and national traditions and customs, any day of the year as United Nations Day for Women's Rights and International Peace and to inform the Secretary-General thereon;

5. *Requests* the Commission on the Status of Women to consider, as a contribution to the preparation of the World Conference of the United Nations Decade for Women, to be held in 1980, the elaboration of a draft declaration on the participation of women in the struggle for the strengthening of international peace and security and against colonialism, racism, racial discrimination, foreign aggression and occupation and all forms of foreign domination and to report thereon to the Economic and Social Council at its sixty-fourth session;

6. *Invites* the Secretary-General to submit to the General Assembly at its thirty-fourth session a progress report on the implementation of resolution 3519 (XXX);

7. *Decides* to include in the provisional agenda of its thirty-fourth session, under the item "United Nations Decade for Women: Equality, Development and Peace", a sub-item entitled "Implementation of General Assembly resolution 3519 (XXX): report of the Secretary-General".

105th plenary meeting
16 December 1977

32/143. Elimination of all forms of religious intolerance

The General Assembly,

Recalling its resolutions 1781 (XVII) of 7 December 1962 and 3069 (XXVIII) of 30 November 1973, as well as its resolution 3267 (XXIX) of 10 December 1974, in which it requested the Commission on Human

[191] *Report of the World Conference of the International Women's Year* (United Nations publication, Sales No. E.76.IV.1), chap. I.
[192] *Ibid.*, chap. II, sect. A.
[193] A/32/211.

UN General Assembly resolution in 1977

The resolution passed by the General Assembly of the UN on *December 16, 1977* said:

> The General Assembly ….. *Invites* all States to proclaim, in accordance with their historical and national traditions and customs, any day of the year as United Nation's Day for Women's Rights and international peace and to inform the Secretary-General thereon….." [91]

Although the resolution said "any day", almost all States of the world, including India, have recognized "March 8" as International Women's Day and have been issuing International Women's Day messages and greetings on March 8 every year.

In 2015, the Women's International Democratic Federation (WIDF) looked back at its seven decades of history and noted, "They were years of many struggles and mobilizations whereupon women of the world and the initiative of our organization in the UN meeting won the establishment of International Women's Day." [92]

Hence it was the socialist as well as the communist women's movement that created the International Women's Day.

It was the communist women's movement that gave birth to the date March 8.

It was the communist women's movement that made March 8 as the permanent date for International Women's Day.

It was the communist women's movement that took the initiative and efforts that paved the way for the UN's celebration of International Women's Day and its passing of the resolution inviting all States to celebrate International Women's Day.

This does not mean that the full credit goes to the communist women's movement alone.

The credit, certainly, goes to non-communist women's movements, organizations, political organizations, the UN and individuals also. We have already seen the contributions of many of them.

> But *the foremost and decisive role* was played by the communist women's movement.

To conclude:

- The real origin of International Women's Day was the resolution of International Socialist Women's Conference in 1910.
- The real origin of 'March 8' was the Russian Revolution begun by women workers on March 8, 1917.
- The real event that established 'March 8' as the permanent date for 'International Women's Day' was the decision of the Communist Women's International Conference in 1921.

To quote the revolutionary woman worker Alekseeva:

> "Let all women join the proletarian family and march hand in hand for a bright future!"

Appendices

1

Myths vs Reality

There are a number of myths and errors about the origins of International Women's Day and March 8 which are so widespread and established than the reality itself!

These myths attribute the origin of March 8 to an imaginary incident in 1857 or 1908.

Similarly errors have occurred about which organization established March 8 as the permanent date for International Women's Day for all countries and when. The erroneously said year was 1910 or 1913 or 1977. The erroneously referred organizations will be seen later.

Origin of March 8

1857

This is the most widespread and reproduced myth.

The myth is, ''International Women's Day, which celebrates women and their struggle for equal rights, is traditionally observed on March 8, in commemoration of a strike by women workers in garment and textile factories in New York City on March 8 1857."[93]

It is mentioned in one of the UN's websites. Well, while it continues in this website, it has been removed from almost all other related websites of the UN, although some other errors still exist there too. But it is still seen in hundreds of articles on internet and in print.

This myth has been so powerful that almost everybody wrote this story adding more and more emotion. The world communist women's movement itself began to believe this story forgetting that 'March 8' is its own creation!

Women's International Democratic Federation (WIDF), which was created by the world communist women's movement, said in 1966, "1857. It is March 8 ... a long procession of poorly dressed women paraded through the streets (of New York). These are workers of garment and textile factories with placards demanding the improvement of their working conditions and recognition of equal rights for American women ... (The police) trampled them and arrested several women …"[94]

> But it is a shocking truth that nothing happened like that actually, which story has been so widespread and written in innumerable articles and books in many languages!

No such writing has ever referred it to any original/reliable source. A writes the story referring it to nothing. B writes the story adding some more, referring it to A. Then C writes the story adding something more referring it to B. Thus it has been rewritten innumerable times referring to any one of the earlier authors!

But we cannot find any reference of strike or struggle on March 8, 1857 at Timeline of labour issues and events at the well researched article at Wikipedia which deals primarily with USA or at any other reliable source.[93]

Then how did this story of 1857 originate and spread?

> It is an irony that this mythical story was first cooked up in 1955 by *L'Humanité,* the newspaper of the French Communist Party then!

This truth was discovered by two French women researchers in the 1970s.

They, Liliane Kandel and Françoise Picq, published their researched article in French in 1982. They said,

> "It was not until 1955 that the legend of 1857 appeared.
>
> " *L'Humanité,* dated March 5, 1955 published a story "(The International Women's Day continues) the fighting tradition of garment workers of New York who struggled on March 8, 1857 demanding elimination of poor working conditions, 10 hour day and recognition of equality of women with men in work. This event produced a great impression and was repeated in 1909, again by the women of New York..... In 1910... C. Zetkin proposed March 8 as the permanent date for International Women's Day. " ...
>
> "The myth therefore seems to spread like wildfire, as if it corresponded to an expectation. Nobody seems to doubt and everyone is working to expand, dress, to clarify that." [94]

What might be the reason for creating this myth? They said,

> "Was it felt necessary to detach the International Women's Day from Soviet history, to give it a more international

origin, older than Bolshevism, also to create the one, more spontaneous than by a decision of a congress or the initiative of women affiliated to parties?

"Was the year 1857 selected as a final tribute to Clara Zetkin who was born that year and who initiated International Women's Day in the international women's socialist movement?"[96]

Thus, this myth of 1857 dominated for about thirty years and still continues to do so to a large extent.

1908

The myth is, "1909: The first National Woman's Day was observed in the United States as February 28. The Socialist Party of America designated this day in honour of the 1908 garment workers' strike in New York, where women protested against working conditions."[97]

This myth can be seen even now in one of the websites of the UN which exclusively deals with events including International Women's Day.

But nothing happened like that in New York in 1908.

Worse, the Communist Party of the Russian Federation itself believes this mythical strike in 1908. Its official website in Russian says even now. "It began on March 8, 1908. At the call of the Social Democratic Women's Organization in New York, more than fifteen thousand women marched through the city demanding shorter working hours, equal pay for equal work with men and women's suffrage."[98]

No article which talks about New York women workers strike in 1908 refers it to any reliable source. For, nothing like that happened.

We cannot see anything like that on the Timeline at *the website of Research Centre on International Ladies' Garments Workers' Union* [99] which was formed in 1900 in New York and on the Timeline of labour issues and events at Wikipedia mentioned earlier.

Establishing March 8

We have already seen in the text of this book about how and when March 8 was established as the permanent date for International Women's Day for all countries.

To quote:

> Before 1917, International Women's Day was celebrated on Sundays. From 1917, it was celebrated in Russia on the fixed date March 8. The Germans did not follow this but celebrated in 1920 on May 9[64], in 1921 on April 3[65], both Sundays.
>
> After the 1921 Communist Women's International Conference's decision—on the proposals of the Bulgarians- International Women's Day on March 8 was a regular feature in the international communist calendar.
>
> But instead of 1921, the year in which March 8 was made permanent has been erroneously mentioned in many articles. The erroneously mentioned year was 1910 or 1913 or 1977. Even the organizations were erroneously mentioned. Let us see this now one by one.

1910

Clara Zetkin, who was the initiator of International Women's Day, had written in 1928, "The Second International Conference of Socialist Women held at Copenhagen in 1910 decided upon March 8 as the International Women's Day which would be a day of united international action."[100]

This is not correct. This might be due to the lapse of her memory. We have already seen that the said conference did not fix any date for International Women's Day.

1913

Alexandra Kollontai also had written erroneously. In her famous article ' International Women's Day ' she had said, "In 1913 International Women's Day was transferred to March 8." [101]

This might also be due to Kollontai's lapse of memory. In Russia, International Women's Day was observed in 1913 on March 2, not on March 8. In 1914 and 1917 and afterwards it was observed on March 8 permanently, only in Russia. We have already seen this.

But Kollontai's statement "In 1913 International Women's Day was transferred to March 8" implies that it applies to all countries. It is not correct.

1977

Citing "Women Watch: International Women's Day". Un.org., retrieved 2012-03-08, Wikipedia article on International Women's Day says, "...1977 when the United Nations General Assembly invited member states to proclaim March 8 as the day for women's rights and world peace."[102]

This is also an error. This has been removed from the said UN website but continues on Wikipedia and in many other articles till date.

2
CHRONOLOGY

August 17, 1907:

First International Conference of Socialist Women held at Stuttgart, Germany. Resolution demanding right to women to vote and to be elected passed.

May 3, 1908

First city level meeting of ' Woman's Day ' held in Chicago, America.

February 28, 1909

First national level demonstration of ' Woman's Day ' held in America.

August 26–27, 1910

The historic resolution to observe International Women's Day, proposed by Clara Zetkin, Kate Dunker and other comrades, passed by the Second International Conference of Socialist Women, held at Copenhagen, Denmark. This is the real origin of International Women's Day.

March 19, 1911

First observation of International Women's Day in Germany, Austria, Switzerland and Denmark.

May 12, 1912

International Women's Day observed in many countries including Germany and Sweden.

March 2, 1913

International Women's Day observed in Russia for the first time

(according to the Julian calendar on February 17, 1913) and in many countries including Germany.

March 8, 1914

International Women's Day observed in Russia in spite of police repression.

July 28, 1914

World War I began.

November 1, 1914

Lenin called to turn the weapons against the government and the bourgeoisie of each country.

March 7, 1915

International Women's Day observed in Switzerland.

March 26–28, 1915

International Conference of Socialist Women held at Bern, Switzerland called on women to act and to demand peace.

March 8, 1917

The historic revolution in Russia was begun by Petrograd women workers on *International Women's Day of Russia* by striking work and rallying on streets demanding bread and peace. (This revolution was called the February revolution according to the Julian calendar.) This is why International

Women's Day is being observed on March 8. This is the real origin of the 'March 8'.

March 16, 1917

Monarchy of Russia overthrown. The revolution, called February Revolution according to the Julian calendar, triumphed.

November 7, 1917

The first socialist revolution of the world, led by Lenin, began in Russia. This is called the November Revolution (October Revolution according to the Julian calendar).

November 8, 1917

The Soviet takes to itself political power. The ministry headed by Lenin formed. Decrees on Peace and Land passed.

1920

'International Women's Day—March 8' was declared a general holiday in Russia.

July 30–August 2, 1920

The first Communist Women's International Conference held in Moscow.

June 9–15, 1921

The historic decision which made 'March 8' as the permanent date for International Women's Day was taken by the Second International Conference of Communist Women held in Moscow. This was the real event that established 'March 8-International Women's Day'.

December 1, 1945

Women's International Democratic Federation was founded.

November 1, 1961

Women went on strike in the US against nuclear weapons and US' war on Vietnam. This agitation was organized by 'Women Strike for Peace'.

1966

National Organization for Women was founded in the US.

1967

New York Radical Women was founded.

March 8, 1968

International Women's Day was celebrated in Chicago by women's liberation organizations.

September 7, 1968

New York Radical Women protested the Miss America Pageant in Atlantic City.

No "bra-burning" but bras, girdles, etc. thrown into a trash can.

1969

Chicago Women's Liberation Union was founded. Hundreds of feminist groups, movements and many journals spread awareness about feminism.

1971

The Bureau of Women's International Democratic Federation at its meeting in Berlin stressed the importance of an international year for the advancement of women.

February 23, 1972

Freda Brown sent a letter to the UN Secretary-General proposing a Women's Year and Convention for elimination of discrimination against women.

March, 1972

Hertta Kuusinen, submitted the Women's International Democratic Federation's proposal for proclamation of an "International Women's Year" at the meeting of the UN's Commission on the Status of Women.

Later the Commission recommended to the General Assembly the proclamation of 1975 as International Women's Year.

December, 1972

The General Assembly of the UN adopted the recommendation and proclaimed 1975 as International Women's Year.

March 8, 1975

For the first time, the UN celebrated International Women's Day.

June 19–July 2, 1975

World Conference of the International Women's Year held in Mexico City.

December 16, 1977

The General Assembly of the UN passed a resolution inviting all states to proclaim any day of the year as United Nation's Day for Women's Rights and International Peace.

February 2, 2015

Women's International Democratic Federation, on the occasion of the 70th year of its foundation, said in its statement that the struggles of "...women of the world and the initiative of our organization at the UN meeting won the establishment of International Women's Day."

References

1. Eleanor Marx, *Report from Great Britain and Ireland to the Delegates of the Brussels International Congress*, 1891,

   https://www.marxists.org/archive/eleanor-marx/1891/brussels-report.htm

2. Karl Marx, *Capital*, Progress Publishers, Moscow, (Year of publication not mentioned), pp. 243–244.
3. Karl Marx, *Karl Marx and Frederick Engels Selected Correspondence*, Foreign Languages Publishing House, Moscow, (Year of Publication not mentioned), pp 179–182.
4. Karl Marx, *Inaugural Address of the International Working Men's Association*, 1864,

   https://www.marxists.org/archive/marx/works/1864/10/27.htm

5. Karl Marx, *Mr. George Howell's History of the International Working-Men's Association*, 1878,

   https://www.marxists.org/archive/marx/works/1878/08/04.htm

6. http:/en.wikipedia.org/wiki/Haymarket_affair;

   http:/en.wikipedia.org/wiki/International_Workers%27_Day

7. https://www.marxists.org/history/international/social-democracy/
8. William Morris. *Impressions of the Paris Congress, Commonweal*, 1889,

   https://www.marxists.org/archive/morris/works/1889/commonweal/07–paris-congress.htm

Tim Davenport, *The Second (Socialist) International (1889–1923)*, http://www.marxisthistory.org/subject/usa/eam/secondinternational.html

9. Trish Corcoran, *Clara Zetkin, Socialism and Women's Liberation*, 2008,

   https://www.greenleft.org.au/node/39309

10. Alexander Trachtenberg, The History of May Day, 1932,

    https://www.marxists.org/subject/mayday/articles/tracht.html

11. Alexandra Kollontai, *International Socialist Conferences of Women Workers*,

    http://www.marxists.org/archive/kollonta/1907/is-conferences.htm#n10

12. https://en.wikipedia.org/wiki/Universal_suffrage

13. Lenin, *The International Socialist Congress in Stuttgart*, 1907,

    https://www.marxists.org/archive/lenin/works/1907/oct/20.htm#bkV13E041

14. *The Great Soviet Encyclopedia*, Third Edition (1970–1979),

    http://encyclopedia2.thefreedictionary.com/Clara+Zetkin

15. Alexandra Kollontai, *Women Workers Struggle For Their Rights*, 1919,

    http://www.marxists.org/archive/kollonta/1919/women-workers/foreword.htm

16. Renée Côté , *La Journée internationale dês femmes ou les vrais dates des mystérieuses origines du 8 de mars jusqu'ici embrouillés, truquées, oubliées : la clef dês énigmes .La vérité historique*, Montreal: Les éditions du remue ménage, 1984, pp. 32–36.

17. ibid., p. 76.

18. ibid., p. 91.

19. ibid., p. 95.

20. ibid., p. 95.

21. Ibid, p. 153.

22. Alexandra Kollontai, *International Socialist Conferences of Women Workers,*

    http://www.marxists.org/archive/kollonta/1907/is-conferences.htm#n10

23. May Wood-Simons, *Report of Socialist Party Delegation and Proceedings of the International Socialist Congress at Copenhagen, 1910,* Printed by H.G.Adair, Chicago, 1910?, pp. 19, 21,

    https://helda.helsinki.fi/bitstream/handle/10138/154637/1814997_a.pdf?sequence=1

24. Dagmar Stuckmann, *Gebt Raum den Frauen-100 Jahre Internationaler Frauentag in Bremen,* Thrun-Verlag Wiesbaden, Wiesbaden, Germany, 2011, p. 47.,

    www.bremer-frauenmuseum.de/.../Frauentag_endgueltig_index.pdf

25. *The Great Soviet Encyclopedia,* Third Edition (1970–1979),

    http://encyclopedia2.thefreedictionary.com/International+Women%27s+Day+March+8

26. Alexandra Kollontai, *International Women's Day,* 1920,

    https://www.marxists.org/archive/kollonta/1920/womens-day.htm

27. Rosa Luxemburg, *Women's Suffrage and Class Struggle,* 1912,

    http://ciml.250x.com/archive/luxemburg-liebknecht/english/rosa_luxemburg_womens_suffrage_and_class_struggle_1912_english.html

28. Silke Neunsinger, *International Women's Day- A Prism for Women's Political Work,* 2010.

    http://www.arbark.se/pdf_wrd/neunsinger-intl-womens-day-a-prism.pdf

29. Rosa Luxemburg, *Women's Suffrage and Class Struggle,* 1912,

    http://ciml.250x.com/archive/luxemburg-liebknecht/english/rosa_luxemburg_womens_suffrage_and_class_struggle_1912_english.html

30. Stalin, *History of the Communist Party of the Soviet Union (Bolsheviks)*, 1939,

https://www.marxists.org/reference/archive/stalin/works/1939/x01/ch04.htm

31. Chatterjee, Choi, *Celebrating Women: Gender, Festival Culture, and Bolshevik Ideology, 1910–1939*, Pittsburgh, Pa: University of Pittsburgh Press, c2002, pp. 21–58.

http://digital.library.pitt.edu/cgi-bin/t/text/text-idx?c=pittpress;cc=pittpress;idno=31735062135326;node=31735062135326%3A1.7; frm=frameset;view=toc

32. https://en.wikipedia.org/wiki/World_War_I

33. Lenin, *The War and Russian Social-Democracy*, 1914,

https://www.marxists.org/archive/lenin/works/1914/sep/28.htm

34. Krupskaya, *Reminiscences of Lenin*, 1933,

https://www.marxists.org/archive/krupskaya/works/rol/rol19.htm

35. Charles Sowerwine, *Femmes Et Le Socialisme*, 1982, p. 148.

https://books.google.co.in/books?id=oxU9AAAAIAAJ&pg=PA147&lpg=PA147&dq=1915+%2B+international+women%27s+day+%2B+switzerland&source=bl&ots=kd6gvoL8ZV&sig=0DSKkBDemES7zHqArEumRFDrg3k&hl=en&sa=X&ved=0CEoQ6AEwB2oVChMIta3st8ODyAIVQ8COCh0Llw7T#v=onepage&q=1915%20%2B%20international%20women's%20day%20%2B%20switzerland&f=false

36. Krupskaya, *Reminiscences of Lenin*, 1933.

https://www.marxists.org/archive/krupskaya/works/rol/rol19.htm

37. *The Maoriland Worker*, dated October 20, 1915,

http://paperspast.natlib.govt.nz/cgi-bin/paperspast?a=d&d=MW19151020.2.32

38. Charles Sowerwine, *Femmes Et Le Socialisme*, 1982, pp. 150, 147

https://books.google.co.in/books?id=oxU9AAAAIAAJ&pg=PA147&lpg=PA147&dq=1915+%2B+international+women%27s+day+%2B+switzerland&source=bl&ots=kd6gvoL8ZV&sig=0DSKkBDemES7zHqArEumRFDrg3k&hl=en&sa=X&ved=0CEoQ6AEwB2oVChMIta3st8ODyAIVQ8COCh0Llw7T#v=onepage&q=1915%20%2B%20international%20women's%20day%20%2B%20switzerland&f=false

39. https://en.wikipedia.org/wiki/Russian_Revolution
40. Brian Baggins, *Timeline of the Russian Revolution (1917).*

    https://www.marxists.org/history/ussr/events/timeline/1917.htm
41. S. Schmidt, K. Tarnovsky, I. Berkhin, *A Short History of the USSR,* Progress Publishers, Moscow, 1987, pp. 123–138.
42. Brian Baggins, *Timeline of the Russian Revolution (1917).*

    https://www.marxists.org/history/ussr/events/timeline/1917.htm
43. S. Schmidt, K. Tarnovsky, I. Berkhin, *A Short History of the USSR,* Progress Publishers, Moscow, 1987, pp. 123–138.
44. Quoted from the Petrograd Soviet newspaper, *Izvestiia,* dated March 3, 1917,

    http://alphahistory.com/russianrevolution/formation-provisional-government-1917/
45. Lenin, *The Tasks of the Proletariat in the Present Revolution [a.k.a. The April Theses],* 1917,

    https://www.marxists.org/archive/lenin/works/1917/apr/04.htm
46. Brian Baggins, *Timeline of the Russian Revolution (1917),*

    https://www.marxists.org/history/ussr/events/timeline/1917.htm
47. S. Schmidt, K. Tarnovsky, I. Berkhin, *A Short History of the USSR,* Progress Publishers, Moscow, 1987, pp. 136–137,

48. Lenin, *Report on Peace*, 1917,

https://www.marxists.org/archive/lenin/works/1917/oct/25–26/26b.htm

49. Lenin, *Report on Land*, 1917,

https://www.marxists.org/archive/lenin/works/1917/oct/25–26/26d.htm

50. Lenin, *Decision to Form the Workers' and Peasants' Government*, 1917,

https://www.marxists.org/archive/lenin/works/1917/oct/25–26/26e.htm

51. John Reed, Ten Days that Shook the World, 1919,

https://www.marxists.org/archive/reed/1919/10days/10days/ch5.htm

52. Рабочий день и рабочая неделя в СССР и России. Досье, 2014,

http://tass.ru/info/1491606

53. Constitution of the Russian Soviet Federated Socialist Republic, 1918,

https://www.marxists.org/history/ussr/government/constitution/1918/article4.htm

54. The Russian Revolution and the Emancipation of Women, *Spartacist*, English Edition No. 59, Spring 2006,

http://www.icl-fi.org/english/esp/59/emancipation.ht

55. КОДЕКС ЗАКОНОВ О ТРУДЕ 1918 года,

http://www.hist.msu.ru/Labour/Law/kodex_18.htm

56. Alexandra Kollontai, T*he Woman Worker and Peasant in Soviet Russia*,

https://www.marxists.org/archive/kollonta/1921/peasant.htm

57. Lenin, *A Great Beginning*, 1919,

https://www.marxists.org/archive/lenin/works/1919/jun/19.htm

58. Alexandra Kollontai, *International Women's Day*, 1920,

http://www.marxists.org/archive/kollonta/1920/womens-day.htm

59. Stalin, *History of the Communist Party of the Soviet Union (Bolsheviks)*, 1939,

https://www.marxists.org/reference/archive/stalin/works/1939/x01/ch07.htm

60. http://encyclopedia2.thefreedictionary.com/Moscow

61. https://en.wikipedia.org/wiki/1st_Congress_of_the_Comintern

62. https://en.wikipedia.org/wiki/2nd_World_Congress_of_the_Comintern

63. R.C. Elwood, Ralph Carter Elwood, Inessa Armand, *Revolutionary and Feminist*, 2002,

https://books.google.co.in/books?id=xXs77PzCaYkC&pg=PA259&lpg=PA259&dq=inessa+armand+%2B+communist+women%27s+international&source=bl&ots=bl_4t9cPWf&sig=5aHKt39dyGiusihE-cFcoG8nfEo&hl=en&sa=X&ved=0CDYQ6AEwCWoVChMIit377f_xyAIVEctjCh0BMg35#v=onepage&q=inessa%20armand%20%2B%20communist%20women's%20international&f=false

64. http://encyclopedia2.thefreedictionary.com/Clara+Zetkin

65. Renée Côté, pp. 163–164.

66. Dagmar Stuckmann, *"Gebt Raum den Frauen" 100 Jahre Internationaler Frauentag in Bremen,*

http://www.bremer-frauenmuseum.de/veroeffentlichungen/Frauentag_endgueltig_index.pdf

67. Gisela Notz, Der Internationale Frauentag und die Gewerkschaften:

Geschichte (n)—Tradition und Aktualität, 2011,

https://frauen.verdi.de/themen/nachrichten/++co++67856fa8–1a33–11e3–8a42–52540059119e

68. ibid.
69. Silke Neunsinger, *International Women's Day—A Prism for Women's Political Work,* 2010,

    http://www.arbark.se/pdf_wrd/neunsinger-intl-womens-day-a-prism.pdf
70. http://encyclopedia2.thefreedictionary.com/International+Women%27s+Day+March+8
71. Ira V. Brown, "Am I Not a Woman and a Sister?" The Anti-Slavery Convention of American Women, 1837–1839, *Pennsylvania History: A Journal of Mid-Atlantic Studies,* Vol. 50, No. 1 (January, 1983), Penn State University Press, pp. 1–2,

    https://journals.psu.edu/phj/article/viewFile/24363/24132
72. https://en.wikipedia.org/wiki/Feminism#Mid-twentieth_century
73. https://en.wikipedia.org/wiki/Seneca_Falls_Convention
74. Clara Zetkin, *Movements for the Emancipation of Women: Three Essays,* Kamgar Prakashan, Delhi, 1988,

    http://www.revolutionarydemocracy.org/archive/zetkin.htm
75. Linda Napikoski, *New York Radical Women—1960s Radical Feminist Group,*

    http://womenshistory.about.com/od/feminism/a/new_york_radical_women.htm
76. http://jewishcurrents.org/september-7–protesting-the-miss-america-pageant-20744#comments
77. CWLU Herstory Editorial Committee, *The Chicago Women's Liberation Union: An Introduction,* 2000,

    http://cwluherstory.org/Historical-Context/
78. Vivian Rothstein and Naomi Weisstein, *Chicago Women's Liberation Union: A Detailed Report of the CWLU's Organizing Strategy,* 1972,

    http://cwluherstory.org/chicago-womens-liberation-union.html

79. http://cwluherstory.org/cwlu-newsletter-march-1968–vol-i-no-1.html

80. Kayomi Wada, *National Black Feminist Organization (1973–1976),*

http://www.blackpast.org/aah/national-black-feminist-organization-1973–1976

81. Raya Dunayevskaya, *Rosa Luxemberg, Women's Liberation and Marx's Philosophy of Revolution,* Humanities Press, New Jersey, 1982, pp. 100–101,

http://abahlali.org/wp-content/uploads/2006/11/raya.pdf

82. http://www.fdimwidf.org/#!8–de-março-Dia-Internacional-da-Mulher-FDIM-70–anos-de-lutas-e-conquistas-1945–2015/c1is6/i74zojo919

83. https://www.marxists.org/history/international/comintern/dissolution.htm

84. S. Penn, J. Massino (ed.), *Gender Politics and Everyday Life in State Socialist Eastern and Central Europe,* Palgrave Macmillan, New York, 2009, p. 63,

https://books.google.co.in/books?id=YaO_AAAAQBAJ&pg=PA63&lpg=PA63&dq=24th+session+of+the+UN+Commission+on+the+Status+of+Women&source=bl&ots=X57ZDgAB-2&sig=QHzYEl6Nw780dX3R7O9F2P5rZWk&hl=en&sa=X&ei=UF7XVLukGdWRuATP64GoDQ&ved=0CEEQ6AEwBg#v=onepage&q=24th%20session%20of%20the%20UN%20Commission%20on%20the%20Status%20of%20Women&f=false

85. http://en.wikipedia.org/wiki/Freda_Brown#cite_note-AW-1

86. http://en.wikipedia.org/wiki/Union_of_Australian_Women

87. Francisca de Haan, A Brief Survey of Women's Rights, *UN Chronicle,* February, 2010,

http://unchronicle.un.org/article/brief-survey-womens-rights/

88. Hilkka Pietilä, *The Unfinished Story of Women and the United Nations,* UN Non-Governmental Liaison Service (NGLS), Geneva, 2007, p. 39,

http://www.un-ngls.org/orf/pdf/UnfinishedStory.pdf

89. S. Penn, J. Massino (ed.), *Gender Politics and Everyday Life in State Socialist Eastern and Central Europe,* Palgrave Macmillan, New York, 2009, pp. 63–64,

    https://books.google.co.in/books?id=YaO_AAAAQBAJ&pg=PA63&lpg=PA63&dq=24th+session+of+the+UN+Commission+on+the+Status+of+Women&source=bl&ots=X57ZDgAB-2&sig=QHzYEl6Nw780dX3R7O9F2P5rZWk&hl=en&sa=X&ei=UF7XVLukGdWRuATP64GoDQ&ved=0CEEQ6AEwBg#v=onepage&q=24th%20session%20of%20the%20UN%20Commission%20on%20the%20Status%20of%20Women&f=false
90. http://www.un.org/events/women/iwd/2008/history.shtml
91. http://www.un.org/documents/ga/res/32/ares32r142.pdf
92. http://www.fdimwidf.org/#!8–de-março-Dia-Internacional-da-Mulher-FDIM-70–anos-de-lutas-e-conquistas-1945–2015/c1is6/i74zojo919
93. http://www.un.org/press/en/1996/19960304.note5322.html
94. "How International Women's Day was Born" in *Women of the Whole World,* Women's International Democratic Federation, Berlin, 1966, No. 1, quoted in Renée Côté, p. 17.
95. https://en.wikipedia.org/wiki/Timeline_of_labor_issues_and_events#cite_note-fillippelli_p020–6
96. Liliane Kandel et Françoise Picq Le mythe des origines, à propos de la journée internationale des femmes 1ère publication: La Revue d'En face, n° 12, automne 1982

    http://www.archivesdufeminisme.fr/ressources-en-ligne/articles-et-comptes-rendus/articles-historiques/kandel-l-journee-des-femmes-le-mythe-des-origines/
97. http://www.un.org/events/women/iwd/2008/history.shtml
98. http://kprf.ru/history/date/116215.html
99. http://ilgwu.ilr.cornell.edu/timeline/
100. Clara Zetkin, *Movements for the Emancipation of Women: Three Essays,* Kamgar Prakashan, Delhi, 1988.

http://www.revolutionarydemocracy.org/archive/zetkin.htm#3

101. Alexandra Kollontai, *International Women's Day* , 1920

https://www.marxists.org/archive/kollonta/1920/womens-day.htm

102. https://en.wikipedia.org/wiki/International_Women%27s_Day